RV CAMPING
Everything I Wish I Knew Earlier

*Practical Trailer Organization
Tricks & Tips for Beginners*

Sara Bowton

DISCLAIMER

This book is based on the experience, opinions, and knowledge of the author and is not intended to be considered a set of instructions. Other products and methods may achieve the same results.

This book includes information about third party services and products. I do not assume responsibility for any third-party materials or opinions. Using any of the mentioned third-party materials does not guarantee your results will mirror those mentioned in the book.

This book is not intended to give legal, financial or cooking advice. The author is not engaged to provide legal, accounting or other professional services or advice. The information is provided "as is", and is to be used at your own risk.

No part of this publication may be reproduced, distributed, or transmitted in any form or by any means, including photocopying, recording, or other electronic or mechanical methods, or by any information storage and retrieval system without the prior written permission of the publisher, except in the case of very brief quotations embodied in critical reviews and certain other noncommercial uses permitted by copyright law.

Table of Contents

WHY I WROTE THIS BOOK

A few years ago, we walked by a campsite with a family that was clearly having their first camping trip. They had clothes piled up, nowhere to properly store dishes. It looked absolutely chaotic, and they were stressed. I stopped and offered some tips.

I came to realize that not everyone has the "camping thing" figured out. Tricks and tips are not always passed on from generation to generation around the campfire, especially for those who have never camped before.

This book is a collection of the best RV advice I learned and still use over the years. After sitting on this information for too long, I finally found a way to share it. This book is the result.

This book is not generalized fluff about camping or tips that are repeated in every other book. They are the methods and tricks we have used for years that have made it much easier to RV camp.

Thank you for buying this book and for letting me share this information with you. I hope the tips, secrets, and tips improve your camping vacations as much as they have helped us.

WHY YOU SHOULD READ THIS BOOK

How many camping vacations do you take each summer? One longer trip, and maybe two more weekend getaways? With few opportunities each year to get it right, it can take many, many years to figure out how to camp efficiently.

With this book, you can fast track your learning process and remove stress from your next camping trip. You will learn the secrets of those in the next campsite who seem to have it all together.

Imagine you are camping and it feels comfortable, easy and enjoyable. Imagine it went so well that you are looking forward to a longer trip next time. Imagine the people in the next campsite are looking at you with envy. This can be your reality.

The keys to an enjoyable camping experience hinge on a few things:

1 – How organized you are and how well you manage your small and outdoor living spaces.

2 - Weather. Sunny is good. Rain, not so good.

3 – Location. Enjoyable scenery and a place with respectful neighbors and light or no traffic is ideal.

4 – Avoid taking a vacation with someone who is clearly a jerk. Spending 24 hours a day in the woods with fewer amenities than you find in your home will not make things better in your relationship. It's like saying we can improve the marriage by deciding to raise donkeys. Not the best idea of the day.

I can't help you with number 2-4 on the list, but I can help with the organization, tips, and tricks.

This book will not tell you which RV to buy. I will not tell you where to find your water intake valve. We will assume that you have that covered from a different book and made an excellent decision and know the basics.

This book is will share the time-tested secrets that have dramatically improved our camping trips. This book will give you secrets such as:

✓ An easy communication trick when parking the RV,
✓ How to prepare an efficient outdoor kitchen,
✓ The secret knob that controls your fridge temperature,
✓ The item saves you 80% on your propane costs,
✓ How to pack clothes for small spaces,
✓ The laundry trick that prevents moldy dirty clothes,
✓ How to maximize your small space,
✓ How to organize your toiletries,
✓ How to extend your grey water tanks,
✓ The key items you need to remember to bring.
✓ The overlooked item needed for electronics.
✓ How to unhitch the trailer when it is stuck on the ball,
✓ Plus, a bonus of easy camping recipes and meal ideas.

Our family has camped for more than 20 years. We have camped for extended periods each summer for more than 10 years. By extended periods, I mean we leave the house and do not return for 35+ days, camping every night. And we don't want to kill each other by the end of it.

Let's make your next camping trip much easier and more enjoyable using clever tips and tricks. Starting now.

TIPS & TRICKS FOR RV CAMPING

HOW TO SAVE YOUR MARRIAGE WHEN BACKING UP YOUR TRAILER OR RV

You spent a week packing up the trailer to make it your enjoyable mini home on wheels. You've locked up the house and just traveled 6 hours to your chosen campground. You finally get to the site, and now you just need to park the trailer.

This is the scene we have seen too frequently at our neighboring campsites.

The passenger (for simplicity, we'll can her Joan) jumps out of the truck and runs to the other end of the campsite to direct the alignment. The driver (named Henry) then begins to back it up.

But Henry has turned too early and is about to hit a tree. Joan, who is unfortunately out of Henry's line of sight begins to wave her hands frantically and scream that he needs to move the back end more to the right. However, Henry cannot see or hear Joan. The location of the truck and trailer during this process are making her frequently invisible and hard to hear.

Henry continues on the current track, unaware of the nearby danger to their 50-thousand-dollar unit (and an innocent tree). A frantic Joan runs to the side of the trailer, waking up the dead with her screaming that he needs to STOP. NOW. Henry stops, drives forward, and then tries backing up again, hopefully this time a bit more to the right. This process repeats until somehow the couple blindly gets the thing into the site.

The solution to this communication problem?

Use your cell phones. In this day and age, both people normally have a cell phone. Jump out of the car and call the driver. If they have blue tooth, it is even easier. Now they can hear you without screaming and without confusing "two more feet" with "look on the street".

Ironically, Joan was probably holding her cell phone just before putting it down to walk to the other end of the campsite to scream at him 30 feet away. Yes, you will often be 30 feet or less apart. But with a trailer and a truck between you, it is 30 feet that needs a communication boost.

The words, *Of Course,* probably appear next in your mind. But amazingly, almost no one uses their cell phones. I know because I always watch as people back into their sites to see if they have figured out this trick. They have not.

In all our years of camping, people use the "scream and wave" method their go-to method of communication. A rare occasion, they use walkie-talkies. Radios are only needed if you don't have cell phone reception at the site.

There is one more important tip to note. BEFORE you start backing up the trailer the driver needs to stop on the road, get out of the vehicle and walk the 15 feet back to the site and survey the situation. This investment can be done in under a minute.

The person should be looking for trees, large rocks or posts (like the campsite number post) that could be a problem – both in the site and on the opposite side of the road. You can hit things with the front of your truck as it swings around when you back up, and the campgrounds often have narrow single-lane roads. Do not underestimate this real hazard, especially as the front of the truck is often a blindspot.

Both people also need to look for the slope of the site, how wide the entrance is, the length of the site and the location of the hookups if the site has them. Both people should agree where the RV should be parked on the site. Never assume you both would agree on the target location any more than you would assume that everyone else likes your favorite pizza topping.

Then when Joan references a tree or rock, Henry has an idea of how big and where the item is actually located relative to everything else. This makes communication much easier. You do not have time to read a descriptive novel of the setting as the driver is backing up.

This is a step that people often think is unnecessary, but it has made a huge difference in lowering our number of attempts when we park. Any time that we have problems getting it right, it is because we got lazy and skipped this step. Ultimately my husband had get out of the truck anyway and survey the land after failed attempt number three, so all we did was prolong our public humiliation and pain. Yes, you should expect that all of your new neighbors will casually observe and evaluate your skillset from their site. Every. Single. Time. In the camping world the most exciting thing on earth is watching someone else trying to back into their campsite.

This 30-second investment can make the difference between a 3-minute good parking experience, and a 30-minute frustrating experience of repeated and embarrassing attempts.

When you use your cell phones and you do a quick sweep of the area before you park, you will look like an expert camper to your many new fans.

Plus, both the tree and the trailer will be saved.

TRAILER STEERING TRICK

If you are struggling to get the back of the trailer to go right or left on demand, here is the trick we learned.

Put your hand on the bottom of the steering wheel (6 o'clock position). If you want the *back end* of the trailer to go right, move your hand (at the bottom of the steering wheel) to the right (towards the 3 o'clock position). And move your hand on the wheel towards the left (towards 9 o'clock position) if you want the *back end* to go left.

Generally, the worst thing you can do when backing up is to turn it too hard initially and jack-knife it. Whenever we have to start over backing it up, the driver had turned too hard initially. We normally start with a small turn as soon as the trailer back end gets close to the driveway and make small adjustments after that. And keep an eye on the front of your truck to make sure you have enough clearance on that end as well as you move.

I would also recommend that you practice a few times in advance in an open area, like a large parking lot or driveaway before you add the challenge of working around trees and tight roads.

CAMPSITE ARRIVAL CHECKLIST

Remember that there is no rush. You can back up more than once to get it right. Once you are in the site:

1 Is the distance to the power and water hookups close enough from your RV to your outlets?

2 Did you give the slides enough space to expand?

3. Do you need to put one side on risers to make it level? If the site is not level side to side about the wheels, it is a good idea to have leveling blocks, which you can buy at any RV dealer, or if you are cheap like is, we use a couple 2x8 pieces that we cut to around 9 inches. You want it as long as possible, but that can still fit between the 2 wheels in the trailer. You put down the wood on the lower side and drive it forward the a few inches inches until the tires are resting on the blocks. This is really important if the site is heavily sloped, or everything will roll to one side and sleeping becomes uncomfortable.

4. Park. Put the chocks for all the tires. (This is not optional. You need to have blocks in place to make sure it does not go anywhere. If you are cheap like us, we made ours out of a mini-tower of 2 x 4s. Have worked great for over a decade.)

5. Disconnect the truck from the trailer, including the hitch, safety wire, chains and bar stabilizers. Bring extra wood to put under the tongue jack so that it does not dig into the dirt and so that it can be raised up higher, if needed. We bring 4-5 blocks that are 4x4 posts cut into about 9 inches in length so that they can be stacked if needed. (and we have almost always needed to stack them to get it level) Also remember to release the ball from the hitch before trying to raise it up.

6. Change the height of the tongue jack so that it is level from the front to the back.

7. Lower your stabilizers.

8. If you have hook ups, connect up to the water, sewer and power outlets.

9. Put out the slides.

10. Take out everything else you need and set up camp – chairs, tables, BBQ, etc.

UNHITCHING THE TRAILER & WHAT TO DO IF YOU CAN NOT GET THE HITCH AND BALL UNSTUCK

You parked the trailer at the campsite. Good job!

The next big hurdle is unhitching the trailer from the truck.

While I mention it briefly in the previous page, you may want to add a few more details to look and feel confident on your gravel pad. Here are the steps we follow to unhitch the trailer:

1 – Block the wheels of the trailer.

2 – Disconnect the electrical plug, the breakaway switch (the very important and thin little cable) and the safety chains.

3 – Use the tongue jack to raise the hitch up a few inches. This is to take weight off the equalizer bars.

4 – Remove the equalizer bars, using the tool included with your trailer. Be careful when you snap the bars down. If there is a lot of tension, they will snap down hard and the handle could go flying or come down hard on your thumb of you are not ready for it. Thus, the importance of step 3.

5- Crank the tongue jack back down, so that the tongue jack is sitting off the ground and all the weight is back to sitting on the hitch.

6- Now release the hitch.

There are times that the hitch does not want to release from the trailer. During our last trip, we met a family who had this problem.

They raised the hitch many inches above the neutral position, I guess trying to have the hitch fall off with gravity. It was to the point that the trailer was sloped severely towards the back and the hitch was high in the air.

This was a big mistake. Leaving it like that could have affected the fridge (it needs to be level when you are using it), and made it impossible to be able to use the truck for their entire trip. Also, sleeping at that angle would have been a challenge. Overall, No Bueno.

If you cannot get it released and it is STUCK on the ball: (technically called the coupler, if you want to have all the technical terms while you are frustrated.)

After completing Steps 1-6, put the truck in drive and move forward about a quarter of an inch (which is about as far as it will go).

If you have been driving for any time, there is a lot of pressure on the ball. We want to interfere with this pressure.

The wheel blocks have locked the trailer so that it won't move forward with the truck when you drive that tiny amount. By moving the truck VERY SLIGHTLY, it takes the pressure off the "coupler lock" and then it should be possible to unhitch the thing.

7 – Once the coupler is released, jack the tongue back up, until the hitch is higher than the ball of the tow vehicle. It must be completely above the ball. Then drive the tow vehicle forward.

8 - Level the trailer as needed depending on the angle of your site.

OUTDOOR KITCHEN ORGANIZATION TIPS, TRICKS AND ESSENTIAL ITEMS

Whenever we see a tour of someone's RV in a video, they always show all their cutlery and plates, cups, etc., neatly tucked in a cupboard and drawer. It always amazes me that this is how they organize their camping kitchen.

The kitchen in any reasonably sized RV is super small. The counter space in my 30-foot trailer is about 8 inches, which is barely enough room to make tea, let alone an entire meal.

I realize that if you have a 45-foot fifth wheel with 8 slides, you will have an island and 35 feet of counter space, where you make daily buffets for your party of 15. But for the common folk, that is not the case.

As a rule, we do NOT make meals in the trailer. We make all meals outside. What if it is raining you ask? Then we either make the meal under a canopy or tarps (discussed later), or we just say, screw it and eat out that meal.

There are many advantages to making all meals outside.

First, this leads to less mess in the trailer. We're looking at spills, crumbs and trying to navigate on multiple surface areas inside the RV. Instead, I clean up by washing the tables, rinsing them off, and turning them on their side for 5 seconds to drain them off.

Second, it gives you more space to work. I have 8 feet of outside counter space using both tables. That beats 8 inches of counter space any day of the week. I am not a super chef who can make 4 different dishes the space of a breadbox. I need room to move, chop, mix. My trailer kitchen stores food but is not the ideal place for my prep work.

Third, since we also eat outside, it is closer to our "dining area". Eating in a trailer at the dinette is not preferable. (see 2 paragraphs up) Unless you are camping in a bubble, you will be sweeping out the dirt daily, if not more often and using a flat mop at least once a day as well. The less frequently you need to clean the floor, the better. This is, after all, supposed to be an enjoyable trip, where you do more than just clean 200 square feet 9 times a day.

If we are not prepping inside, it means that we need to have an outdoor kitchen. This is how we set up ours to be as functional as possible.

a) Collapsible tables for food prep. I personally use two tables. Each table is four feet long. The legs fold down and they cost about $50 each. They are stored stacked in the trailer on travel days. I make them into an "L" formation and use one for meal prep and one for temporary food storage.

If you are staying at a campsite or RV park with tighter spacing, you could put the tables up against the trailer, and if it is a really tight site, use one table instead of 2.

b) Clear plastic containers with lids for plates and cups. While your trailer looks sparkling clean in the showroom, remember that you are moving your trailer to a location full of dirt, bugs, and more dirt. I got my containers from the Dollar Store. They are about 10 inches by 18 inches. One holds cups, and one holds plates. I chose see-thru plastic to make it easy to see which is which and put a label on the top and side of the box to make it super clear. I use another smaller plastic container for larger utensils, such as a ladle, spatula, peeler, large knife, cheese grater, and such.

c) Cutlery Plastic Cases. I have used children's pencil cases (the rectangular ones with a flip-over lid) or smaller plastic containers with a lid (both from the Dollar Store, yes there is a cheap solution theme here) for the cutlery. Again, we use two containers. I sort them with one for knives, and one for forks and spoons. I am not in the mood to stop and clean cutlery halfway through the process, so I bring a dozen or more of each cutlery type. Without 2 containers, the extra cutlery could make 1 container too full. Also, it's easier to find an item that way.

The need for reasonable sized plastic containers cannot be understated if you plan to do your cooking outdoors. When we arrive, we take all the boxes out at the same time and put them on a table. We often leave them on the picnic table between uses since everything is clean and protected from the elements, thanks to the lids

One caveat is if you are camping in a place where you don't trust the neighbors not to help themselves to your stuff while you are away. Then obviously bring in the collection when not in use. It still only takes seconds to move the stack in and out of the trailer when needed if you feel more comfortable bringing it in between meals.

d) Bar-B-Q. If you have a newer trailer with a built-in BBQ, you are already set. If not, you need to get a tabletop or collapsible BBQ. We have a small folding table to hold our BBQ. You can also use your picnic table, but then you lose space for eating.

The BBQ is used for almost all meals. It is basically a substitute oven. If you don't have an electrical hook up, we use it to make up to 8 slices of toast at a time. The BBQ is used in almost all meals. This item is considered essential.

e) Propane Stove. Most trailers have a hook up for an outdoor propane stove. If you don't, you will need to get a stovetop one. Often you even find a second hand one online.

The inside trailer stove is to be used for emergencies, such as it is freezing outside one morning and you want to boil water for coffee. Then you use the indoor stove to allow you to make the coffee without venturing into the arctic air, and warm-up the trailer so that you will get the courage to strip down and change into your clothes for the morning.

f) 1 to 20 Pound Converter Propane Adapter Hose. This item is directly related to items (d) and (e). If you have a tabletop stove or BBQ, you will need propane, of course. Those little bottles of propane can easily deplete a bank account as they are $6 or more for each 1-pound container of propane.

But there is hope on the horizon. You can get an adapter at Wal-Mart or a hardware store that converts the stove/BBQ connection from requiring to use only the tiny canisters to now be able to use the 20-pound tanks. It costs about $30 but it will pay for itself very quickly. This changes the price from six dollars or more per pound to about a dollar a pound, which is over an 80% discount on your propane costs.

Then you can just bring the 20-pound tank with you, (or take the extra tank off your trailer if the trailer holds 2 and you are completely out), and hook it up and voila! Propane at a fraction of the cost. We have found that a 20-pound tank can last us up to 5 weeks of daily use, even when we use it for multiple meals each day.

g) French Press Coffeemaker. If you don't have an electrical hook up, a coffeemaker is not an option, and either way, it can be bulky.

We use a French press to make coffee. It takes up much less space, makes coffee in under a minute after the water boils, and works under all conditions. It costs about $15 and available in most kitchenware aisles. I have even found them at the Dollar Store for only a couple of bucks.

h) Dishwashing basins. After you make the mess you have the joy of cleaning it up. Here if you have full hookups, including sewer, you have the choice of bringing all the dirty dishes inside, washing, rinsing and drying them, and then putting them back in their bins.

However, if you don't have unlimited sewer capacity or don't want the hassle of bringing dirty dishes inside the trailer, here is what we do.

We have 2 plastic tubs from the Dollar Store. They are made with thicker plastic, and I think sometimes they even say wash bins on their label. You want ones that can handle heavyweight, as water is not light.

One of the bins is for washing the dishes and the other is for rinsing. I prefer round ones to square because they fit easier in my sink when filling.

The washing bins have multiple purposes. We use them during meal prep to bring out (and bring back in) the assortment of food and spices you need to take out of the cupboards and fridge. This works better than trying to fit it all in your arms and dropping the pickles all over your last pair of clean socks.

Even if we have full hookups, we still wash, rinse and dry the dishes outside. We want the extra space outside to give enough room to the helpers. Plus, since all the dishes are stored in bins that are already outside, it is easier to put them away.

One more thing...washing dishes with a lot of "stuff" on them is not fun on the best of days. It makes the dishwater turn very unpleasant in a hurry.

To address this, we wipe down the plates and bowls when there is a lot of mess (think spaghetti sauce, mustard, ketchup, salad dressing, BBQ sauce, etc.) with paper towels or Kleenex prior to putting the extra messy plates or bowls in the dishwater. We will either throw the dirty tissues in the garbage or use them to start the fire later that day.

Bring an extra Kleenex and or/paper towel roll to handle the increased demand. It may not be the most fun thing to do upfront, but it makes it easier to wash everything without having to change the wash water several times.

i) Coolers – Extend Your Fridge Space. I bring an extra cooler for all beverages. We fill the cooler with a bag of ice each day and it keeps everything cold, and easily available without using valuable and very limited fridge space. This gives us several more cubic feet of useable space without forcing people to have lukewarm drinks.

j) Sorting Food by Meals. It is easier to sort the foods in your trailer according to the most-used-for-meal type. For us, breakfast has more food variety than you would think. For example, in one plastic milk crate we store bread, peanut butter, honey, oats, sugar, coffee. It makes it easy to just need to grab the cream in the morning, throw it in the box with the rest of the breakfast items and take it outside. It is also easier when you are bringing it all back inside at the end of the meal.

k) If there is no room for an outdoor kitchen of any kind. You have to do the entire meal prep inside. If you have an electrical hook up, I would use a crock-pot whenever possible. It allows you to do the majority of the meal prep in advance. It would also minimize the number of extra pots you have to clean. And you can heat up the leftovers the next night.

THE SECRET RV FRIDGE TEMPERATURE CONTROL LOCATION

I have yet to meet anyone who knows this trick, but it works.

RV fridges generally do not have a temperature control knob, at least not one that is well-known.

However, there is a way to control the temperature of your fridge if you have a fridge with the steel fins as your cooling device. (The fridges with the thin columns of steel above the top row of the fridge to cool the unit.) These are the most popular type of RV fridges.

Look at the steel fin on the far-right side. There, you will find a clear or white plastic bar attached to the plate. That is, amazingly enough, the way to control the fridge temperature. The further up you move the plastic bar on the plate, the colder the fridge will get.

So, if the fridge is too warm, move it up. If the milk starts freezing, move it down a bit. It also controls the freezer temperature.

Before we learned this trick, we had the bar at the bottom of the steel column, not knowing better.

Like almost everyone else, we didn't even realize it was there and certainly had no idea of its true purpose. We also had all sorts of issues with food not keeping as long as we would like and ice cream being too soft.

After learning of this trick and we moved that little plastic bar up the plate. The food lasted much longer and we had, for the first time ever, hard ice cream.

FIND YOUR FAVORITE SHIRT ON DEMAND

Because we have 5 people sharing 200 square feet of interior space, we only have room for one shelf for each person. We have sorted them further with collapsible bins (about 11 x 11 x 11 inches from the Dollar Store) on the shelves. We fit 2 bins on each shelf (measure first to figure it out for you).

One bin is for shirts and shorts and one is for pants and sweaters. You just pull out the bin to get to the clothes and you don't have to reach into a long dark shelf and guess what you are pulling out. It is also easier when putting away your clean clothes.

Even with the shelves in cupboards for larger clothing items, I still use clear plastic containers with lids or an extra drawer for undies, socks and bathing suits. You may be able to combine 2 people's stuff together, depending on the number of days of clothing you pack.

If you roll the clothes you can fit it all in easier and it is also easier to find what you are looking for without messing up the rest of the contents.

Plus, the containers are stackable and keep out the dust and water. Stackable allows for better use of vertical space, which in a trailer, is essential.

ULTIMATE LAUNDRY TRICKS

Regardless if you plan to wash your clothes on your camping trip or you wait until you get home to do it, laundry still needs to be managed. Here's our secret.

Use old pillowcases, or buy some cheap ones and use those for laundry bags. This has several advantages.

The pillowcases allow air to pass through better, unlike garbage bags. So damp clothes are less likely to get funky or moldy if left there for a few days.

Pillowcases can hold a lot of weight. Garbage bags will start stretching as the bag gets full if you need to lift it, and then you have the real possibility that it will tear and drop clothes everywhere before it reaches the washing machine. Not fun.

Plus, you can dump out the contents of the pillowcase without having to touch them. I do not love touching damp dirty clothes that have been sitting there for 5 days. I suspect we have this in common.

I add the used pillowcase "bags" to my wash with the dirty clothes. That way I have a clean bag to bring all the clothes back to the trailer (if I wash them on the trip). And it's environmentally-friendly to boot.

As a reference, if we are gone for 14 days, I will have 6 pillowcases of laundry. For 7 days I will collect 4 pillowcases worth because we will wash towels on laundry day and they use up at least 1 full pillowcase all by themselves.

Bring half a dozen with you, especially if traveling as a family.

Show Me The Money (Bag). I carry an older cloth or leather pencil case with a zipper to hold all my loose change for the laundromat. The one I have is opaque, so no one else can see what is inside. It is also a very durable weave so that it won't break open easily. Finally, I chose a bright red color, so that I can find it fast and it makes it harder to overlook and leave it behind.

Whenever we get some change in dollars or quarters, I put them in the pencil case change holder and store it in the same place every time. We will also get a roll or two of quarters and loonies before a longer trip if I don't have at least $30 in change in the bag.

Laundry Baskets. We only do laundry on the road if we are going on trips longer than 12-14 days. An often-overlooked item is the humble laundry basket.

If you are on a longer trip, laundry on the road is unavoidable. You will be bringing back most of your washed clothes to your campsite in sparkling clean pillowcases, but you will miss the laundry basket in this process, used to transfer the wet clothes to the dryer or the outside drying line.

We use a collapsible rectangular container as a laundry basket. The brand we use is Clever Crates, if you need to see an example. It folds flat to be about 2 inches thick, so you can easily store it on its side when not in use.

Using a basket to transfer clothes to the dryer will reduce the odds that some of the clothes will hit the floor of the questionably clean laundromat. It is also great for keeping together all the clothes that will be hung up at the campsite.

We also will use it to stack the clothes we folded at the laundromat, so that they don't get messed up, and stay sorted.

There may also come times you need a ready on-demand storage box – to transfer groceries or whatever. I have yet to regret bringing it.

As a side note, I often see people in the laundromat, who are only camping for a total of 5 days. I don't want to waste a full morning for laundry if it can at all be avoided.

But if doing laundry throughout the week is your thing, then live your dream. I just recommend you really think if this is how you want to spend an afternoon of a precious 5-day or 3-day trip, especially if it is nice outside.

MAXIMIZING YOUR SMALL SPACE

As you have or will quickly become painfully aware, the amount of space in a trailer, regardless of the size, it is extremely limited. This means that you need to maximize vertical space whenever you can. Look at the layout and the walls for where you can increase the wall space to maximize your storage.

One way is to stick on hooks. You want a brand that can take a fair bit of weight and won't peel off after 4 days. We use Command Hooks™, and they work well. For coats and clothes, and even small bags of fruit we use the 3-pound size without issues as of yet.

If you don't know about these bad boys, you stick them on and can take them off without damaging your walls. I use the hooks for the many coats we have. I have more hooks by the beds for clothes that we plan to wear for a second day, because we are, after all, camping, but still want to keep them off the floor.

They also have the Command Hook™ broom holders. Before we put up the broom holders, the broom was leaning against a wall, waiting to fall on you, and generally in the way. Now we have a holder at each door so that we can put it away easily.

Sort everything possible into bins or containers with lids (and label them). Things can only be put away if they have a home to go to. If all items are sorted into logical bins with labels, they can be stacked and easy to find.

For all toiletries not used on a daily basis, medicines (aspirin, etc.) and first aid stuff, I sort them in clear small plastic containers with lids, that can again be stacked. I have 4 small containers to handle this, which fit easily on one shelf when stacked.

Finally, look for places that are not being used frequently for their intended purpose, such as the microwave and oven. I rarely if ever use either. They are great, self-contained storage units for food items with no other home, such as buns and bread.

ORGANIZING TOILETRIES

When we don't have full hookups, we camp at places with shower facilities. I know, it is not exactly roughing it to the max, but I never said this was survivalist training.

To make it as easy as possible to keep track of all supplies for personal hygiene, I put everything I need in one basket, and have a separate basket for each person. This basket needs to be not too long or wide, but deeper so that the shampoo bottles do not fall over in storage or in transport.

I recommend that the container has some holes in the bottom so that if the bottles get wet, there is airflow. I also will put a facecloth on the bottom to absorb any water from the bottles that can be changed out as needed.

I have a separate basket and personalized toiletry set for each individual. Yes, that means we have duplicates of soap, shampoo, etc., but it allows everyone to shower at the same time, (as long as there are multiple stalls, which there normally are). You also can use partially filled bottles of shampoo etc., for shorter vacations and to decrease the amount of weight you are carrying to the washroom.

In my basket, I have shampoo, conditioner, soap, face wash, moisturizer, toothbrush (in a travel holder), toothpaste, and a razor. I roll up my towel and put it on top. I can walk down to the washroom; everything is tucked together and easy to pick up and go. Before leaving the washroom, I re-roll the towel, put it back on top of the basket.

For some unknown reason, I see people who go into these public showers and do not wear shower shoes. Mind-boggling.

Let us not overestimate how frequently or how well the shower stalls and the floors to the public washrooms are cleaned. In addition, if they last cleaned them at 2 pm and it's now 7 pm, you are far from the first person to shower or enter the washroom after it has been cleaned. Campground washrooms are extremely busy. There has been a lot of dirt and God-only-knows what is on that floor.

As an example, on my last trip, I saw two women in the washroom who showered without shoes. They then walked all around the washroom which was lined in dirt after they got out of the shower. Then they took their ONLY towel and wiped off their feet before putting on their running shoes.

That is something that cannot be unseen. It was the only towel each person brought and they will probably use it again the next night. It now has swipes of dirt off a public bathroom floor all over it. This would be one of the few times that I would recommend NOT showering for the rest of the trip.

REDUCE RV DIRT SIMPLY

If you do not yet have an outdoor RV mat, I would strongly recommend one. We have 2 because we have a longer trailer and two doors. It provides a filter between the abundance of campsite dirt and the floor of your trailer.

We will sweep off the mats daily as well, to keep down the amount of dirt and rocks collecting on them. They cost about $40 if you look at Costco or Wal-Mart. They are more than double at RV dealers if you go that route.

RAIN (AND SUN) PROTECTION

Perhaps every time you go camping the sun will always be shining and it will not be too hot out. We have not had such consistent luck. We plan our camping trips to places with the most likelihood of having good weather. Still, we have camped too many days in rainstorms, full-on rain, drizzle, freezing overnights and temperatures that climb to where you are certain that you have entered an oven from hell in the direct sun.

In those cases, in order to survive and not kill each other from absolute discomfort, tarps and/or canopies come to the rescue.

If you use tarps, you need to figure out how to jerry-rig a series of ropes of various lengths to the trees nearby. Plan for A LOT of longer ropes and when in storage, wind them up on empty water bottles or something similar to prevent re-experiencing the frustration of sorting out a mess of Christmas light cords at a campsite.

Tarps are useful in that you can redirect water to where you want on your site. You can also shift them to block out light if it is too hot in full sun. However, pay attention to ensure they are not too low or decreasing airflow. You should plan for a small ladder (a three-step is a minimum) to reach the needed height, and it helps to bring a tall person.

If you use a canopy, the need for the ropes and acrobatics in the trees goes down. But there are limitations with canopies.

The size of the canopy cover will be generally smaller than the tarps. We normally place the canopy over the picnic table. It will cover the table and a couple feet past it, but not much more.

If there are no additional tarps and it rains, the water will be falling right outside the picnic area. If it is heavy rain, and all you have is the canopy, do not be surprised if the water flows back into the picnic table area.

So why have a canopy? It is fast to set up and you can use it in the absence of trees (which can often be the case). Most have a removable wall on one side. You can quickly put up the wall when it rains to direct the water away from the area on that side (if you have your meal prep area moved to under the canopy).

The removable wall is also a Godsend when you need to block out the direct scorching sun, which makes a HUGE difference. This is especially the case when you are trying to eat supper and the direct sun is pointing like a laser at your picnic table. I speak from experience.

A side note on canopies. The first one we bought had a full screen all the way around. The lack of airflow makes it hotter inside than it is outside. And for some reason, the screen tent attracted every bug within a mile radius to INSIDE the unit. It was like a bottleneck and it was impossible for these flying insects (think wasps) to find their way back outside. It quickly became a hot bug shelter and it was not super fun. We promptly returned it when we got home.

The best canopy version we found had a roof and one removable wall. This allows the flexibility of airflow, shelter from things falling overhead – both water and things from the trees (i.e., bugs, leaves, small branches). It also gives you the option to further block out the direct sun when needed where you get afternoon full sun and it's really hot out.

Luckily these are very common to find in any store with camping equipment. They tend to start at around $100.

NOTES FOR UNSERVICED CAMPSITES

During one of our many longer camping trips, we were moving to a new location and our procedure is to empty the grey water tanks on travel days. This campground had no services, and we had just stayed there 14 nights. This was the first time we emptied the grey water tanks at that campground.

There was a fair lineup so we ended up talking to others in the line. The guy behind us told me that he empties the grey water tanks every 2-3 days. In my humble opinion, it is crazy to use up that much time of your vacation to do this task repeatedly. There are ways to decrease the number of visits required to the least enjoyable location of the campground.

To illustrate, let's go over the steps involved in emptying the grey and blackwater tanks in the middle of a camping trip:

1 - pack at least half the stuff up (everything loose in the trailer),

2 - hitch up the trailer,

3 - sit in line to dump it (especially if it's a popular campground, this can take 1.5 hours or more),

4 - wait 20 minutes to dump when it is your turn,

5 - park the trailer again (often backing it in again)

6 - unpack the stuff you repacked.

Seriously, this guy was repeating this every 2-3 days? The majority of his afternoon is wasted on this one activity. This is not an activity that I personally want to experience any more than necessary.

When we told him that we were going 14 days between grey water dumps, he looked like I said I just flew in on my personal jetpack. Yet, this is definitely possible, and even realistic. Here is how we do it (and have done it every single time).

TIPS FOR EXTENDING YOUR GREY WATER TANKS

For people with better things to do than meet new friends in the dump station line-up, it is possible, with just a few adjustments, to minimize your time there.

Remember those washbasins I referenced earlier? Here they are not optional if you want to extend your grey water tanks. We empty the washbasins in the trees outside the campsite (use biodegradable soap), or at the campground sinks for dishwashing, or dump it down the toilet. But if we are dry camping, we do not fill the greywater tanks with dishwater.

We also minimize greywater in meal prep. When we wash fruit or vegetables, we fill a 2 litre or half-gallon juice jug with water and wash the veggies outside. Just bring a strainer or colander to make it easier – plus it is a place for the veggies to dry off.

All campsites have public washrooms. If you are dry camping, these are your only real options. We go there for the bathroom, showering and while you are there anyway and have it all in your handy toiletry basket, might as well brush your teeth as well.

This means that grey water tanks are mostly getting filled from the rare times you wash your hands or veggies at the kitchen sink and very few other times.

By following this diligently, even as a family of five, we can make one 35-gallon grey water tank last 14 or more days. In fact, we have NEVER emptied a grey water tank during a camping stay by following these rules. We only empty it on travel days.

Plus use the overlooked feature that will extend your grey water tanks...

OVERLOOKED FEATURE
TO EXTEND YOUR GREY WATER TANK

If you plan to ever dry camp, there is one important, yet often overlooked feature on most trailers and RVs that is essential to extend the lifespan of your grey water tank.

The outdoor shower. I have yet to find another resource mention how an outdoor shower can be a game-changer to accomplish this task. This is a huge tip.

If you have one on your RV, for the love of all that is good, USE IT. We had one on both our tent trailer and a full-sized trailer. I can tell you that there is NO WAY that I would even consider a trailer without one. It is a must-have.

To optimize the use of the outdoor shower, we create a wash station. We set up our three-step or two-step ladder beside the showerhead. (The same one you might need for your tarps. Double use everything.)

These ladders have a top handle to grab them. We use the handle to hold a hand towel over top. The top step is where we store the liquid soap dispenser. (We have one liquid soap container inside and a second one outside the trailer.)

The wash station is set up from 10 minutes after we arrive and is in place until 5 minutes before we pack out. Everyone then uses that station for washing hands, face, feet (think sand after going to the beach) and dogs. Plus, people are not going in the trailer with their shoes on and making your floor dirty just to wash their hands.

If we are on a travel day and camping in a rest stop, we will whip open the outdoor shower to wash up in the morning and night.

This saves precious grey water space and does not muck up the kitchen area, especially since the sink is full of items that are secured there for travel days.

In the event that you do not have an outdoor shower attached to your trailer, you can makeshift a portable shower unit, hook it up to the trailer or a tree and still follow the same principles. Not as convenient, but it is still doable.

Either way, washing everything possible outside the trailer using the outdoor shower decreases the flow to the grey water tanks substantially.

REFILLING WATER
WITHOUT MOVING THE TRAILER

While we can maximize the time on the grey water tanks, it does not minimize the need for freshwater. I know there must be a family of 10 that is saving the world by using no more than half a cup of water a day while camping. We will not be getting that award. We use water as needed, recognizing that it is work to refill it.

This means that as a family of 5, we use about 30 gallons of water every couple of days. Since our freshwater tank is about 40 gallons, one fill is not going to cut it for a 14 or even 7-day camping trip. Water refills will be necessary. The way I see you have 3 choices to refill your water:

1- Follow the same steps as the guy I met at the sewage dump station and fill your water there every 48 hours. We've already covered how much fun you should expect to experience.

2- Only camp directly next to a water station that has a tap and get a really long hose. (which severely limits your campsite options).

3- Our method.

We bring 2-3 empty 5- gallon containers just for water refills. If you want to conserve space, they have rectangular space-saving ones if you look around. If you don't care about saving those inches, you can just use the water station refill ones you find at your grocery store.

We store them in a lower cabinet or in the shower. To refill the water, you take your handy empty jugs to the water station in the campground - there are normally several in each campground.

Unless it happens to be very close, we will throw them in the back of the truck and drive over to it, since each one will be 50 pounds heavier on the way back.

The next step is to transfer the water into the freshwater tank.

To do this, we have the largest funnel we could find WITH A FLEXIBLE HOSE. As you can see with the all caps, this is a very important detail. You can often get them in the automotive section of a store, or an automotive store.

The freshwater intake is on the side of the trailer and we need to pour the water from the containers into the side of a wall. This is near impossible to redirect it in without a funnel. The flexible hose is needed to prevent A LOT of spilling and swearing.

If the person is super strong, he/she might be able to hold the 5 gallons in one hand and the funnel in the other (especially after it is down to half full). But you should plan to have 2 people doing this. But seriously, what were the kids doing at that time anyway? They are fully equipped to hold a funnel for 5 minutes.

We tend to top up the freshwater every 2-3 days. This means there are at least 2 round-trip refills each time. The entire process takes about 20 minutes, which beats 3+ hours and all the rest of the hassles any day of the week.

DRINKING WATER OPTIONS

Regardless of how you choose to address the drinking water challenge, recognize that not all water in all places may the quality that you enjoy at home. Prepare for the worst-case scenario -water is not optional. As such, take steps to bring it up to a standard that makes it safe to drink.

We do not drink the water directly from the campsites, even if it says it's ok. This is just not a risk we want to take.

We have a couple of choices for our drinking water. This is not an exhaustive list; it the very short list of how we have handled it.

1 – We get several 5-gallon water jugs and fill them at the supermarket water refilling station every few days. We also pour the water from the large 5-gallon jug into a 2-gallon dispenser, refilling as needed.

2 – We bought a Berkey water filter. We use this at home and when camping. It is a gravity water filter that gets rid of 99.9% of everything, even chemicals. It is several hundred dollars up front, but the filters last 10 years or more, so it saves money in the long end. Then we drink the campsite water, but only after it has been filtered. If you decide to get one, the "Big Berkey" size works for our family, and we drink a lot of water. We also are good with 2 filters and didn't get buy the additional filters (you can use up to 4 at once).

We use a different color water bottle for each person and keep them in the ice-filled cooler I mentioned earlier for cold water on demand.

ENJOYING THE DUMP STATION

You may think that there is nothing unique I can share with you about how to empty a grey and black water tank, but hold on to your shorts, you might just be surprised.

This is not an enviable task. No one will be lined up trying to take the job away from you. But at some point, you will need to do it.

First the basics. If you do use the toilet and need to empty the black water, empty that one first. Then you can "flush" out the hose with the greywater next. Also, if you have the extra water, you might want to fill the toilet with extra water when you are emptying the black water to help rinse it out.

Most people get super long rubber gloves – the ones that go mid-arm, or in some cases, all the way to the elbow. In the end, they stuff the huge, bulky and dirty gloves into the holder with the sewage pipe.

After one has used these gloves once and shoved them into a small dark hole to be stored with the end of a sewage hose for days to weeks, I have no intention of ever touching those things again.

Our solution. We have a large box of disposable gloves stored in an outdoor storage compartment. We grab two from the box and then throw them in the garbage located with the dump stations.

Now every time is like the first time.

HOW TO AVOID:
OMG WHAT IS THAT SMELL?

If you choose to use the trailer toilet this is an essential item. Maybe you are using it for emergencies, or you have full hookups and you are using the facilities regularly. Either way, the odor will permeate if not treated correctly.

There are several options to treat the blackwater tank. There are not environmentally-friendly chemical solutions and some biodegradable solutions.

We have recently started using a product called *Happy Camper™*, which is biodegradable and uses enzymes to loosen up the stuck on "gunk", we will tastefully call it. It is available through RV dealerships and on Amazon. We use 1 "treatment" about every 3-4 days (using full hookups), or each time we empty the black water tank. This really helps prevent the trailer from smelling like a septic tank.

This is necessary even if you have full hookups. Trust me.

Timing is important - when to dump the black water tank. Even with full hookups, you want to wait to dump the black water tank until it is about 2/3 full. You need enough liquid in the tank to flush out the solids, or you will just have a huge clump of dump in your tank at the end of the day.

And always dump the black water first, then the greywater to "rinse" out the sewage hose before you store it again.

When you dump the sewage at the end of the trip, if you did use the toilet, be prepared that you may (likely) need to run the hose to the toilet and just keep flushing until everything is cleaned out and the water runs clear. This may be the case even if you had full hookups. Just sayin'.

HOW TO CHARGE YOUR ELECTRONICS WITHOUT A FULL PLUG-IN OUTLET

Camping for more than a few days at an unserviced campsite will draw down the batteries to nothing if you do not have a way to recharge them.

This is especially the case if you need to charge an assortment of phones, tablets, games, and laptops. Or if it is cold at night and you need to run the furnace regularly, (which means the furnace fan) it will also take the battery into a nosedive.

Regular plugin outlets only work if you have an electrical hookup or when you are running a generator. We charge items all day (and especially while we sleep). This means we are charging at unserviced campsites outside of generator hours. Luckily there is a device that allows this to happen, and as a bonus, it allows you to charge up to 6 devices at once.

A car power inverter. The one I am referring to is often called something like "12V to 110 AC car power inverter". They are available through Amazon and probably at your local automotive store, and start at around $30. I have no idea how we would function without this little unit considering the number of electronics we use for 5 people.

These inverters often have additional charging outlets (we have seen up to six), so you can charge everyone's stuff at once, and it can be used anytime because it uses the battery for a power source.

Next, you need a top-up for a power source. We have both a generator and solar panels.

Solar panels work great in full sun, but if you camp where there is any shade or it is cloudy, the returns diminish quickly. We use them, but we know that the solar panels alone normally will not handle our full power needs for extended periods. The ones we use are not attached to the roof, so we can move them to follow the sun throughout the day to improve the power generation. They cost about $200 on sale for a decent wattage but compact enough panel size. As a reference, we have three 40-watt panels.

Generators will give you the punch you need to get the power topped up. However, they are noisy. In many campgrounds, there are limited hours when they can use them. We use the generator whenever we are at the campsite during generator hours and that is enough to keep the battery at close to full charge. Also, remember that you need to bring a jerry can for gas – you should expect to refill the gas supply after a few days.

Inverter generators are quieter than regular generators, but they cost more. If you have the cash, they certainly make the experience more enjoyable, as the basic generator can be quite loud.

Always keep the generator away from the RV – do NOT put the generator under the RV! Keep the direction of the exhaust away from windows and doors. Generators create exhaust, and you do not want it going into your trailer.

Always lock your generator to something to discourage someone from stealing it. (We normally choose a large tree.) Generators are expensive and valuable.

ESSENTIAL EMERGENCY CLEANING ITEM

There is one item we have in our truck under the driver's seat at all times for emergencies. We do not go through them quickly, so one container will last a long time, but when you need it, you need it.

It is **baby wipes**. Yep, those things advertised to clean your baby's bottom when changing diapers. They won't tear easily, are compact and whatever they use for cleaning agents in them can clean almost anything off of anything. They are essential for emergency hand washing.

Here are some times they will be helpful: After you finish using the dump station, even with your gloves on, things may not always go as well as planned. The last thing you want to do is grip your steering wheel and drive 3 hours under those conditions.

Some more examples of when they are valued. You take a bathroom break on the road in facilities that were cleaned at the turn of the last century and there was no soap. Or the rest stop was an outhouse. Or the dogs/kids got car sick on the ride down and vomited all over the car mats (yep, it happened).

They have also worked when the electrical connector has debris or rust on it. The wipes took the corroded rust off the connector and we drove the trailer home.

I have never used these as actually baby wipes on my kids but I always have a container for emergency cleaning situations.

OTHER KEY ITEMS TO REMEMBER

Elastics. I bring a bunch in a Ziplock bag. The elastics are great for sealing plastic bags or cling wrap to the ends of cheese, veggies, and such. There are a million other reasons to use elastics, which could be listed to create the most boring book in the world, so I'll assume you can take it from here.

Clips. (to close bags) Binder clips (they look black squares with chrome clip ends and can get them in any office supply store to holds stacks of paper together) are perfect to stop anything from chips to marshmallows from spilling everywhere. Plus, when you fold the top of the bag over and then clamp it, it can deter bugs from finding a new home in your food. I bring at least half a dozen to save me a ton of frustration. You can find them at the Dollar Store, kitchenware store or stationery store, depending on your budget and style.

Cutting Boards. If you forget to bring these, you will be preparing a lot of food on your plates, because you quickly realize that both the direct surface of the picnic table and the foldable tables you brought are not options. I bring a few thin flexible ones (from the Dollar Store) and a couple of solid ones (think wood or thick plastic) for good measure.

Ziplock bags. Super helpful. I will spare you the details of how a bag works. We also use them to cap the end of a cheese block or cucumber, etc. and seal it with the elastics you remembered to bring. It can replace plastic wrap in most cases.

Fold-Over Sandwich bags. We also will use these to separate individual hamburger patties, if you want to make them yourself. Then you can take out the exact number you need without worrying about them sticking together. Also great for end caps of long items when you don't want to use a Ziplock bag.

Lysol wipes. This adds to the cleanliness issue. I wipe down the entire picnic table AND picnic seat with several disinfectant wipes. I will not tell you the amount of dirt and God-knows-what is picked up when I do this but, it is more than you want to know.

I have heard of some people actually putting their sewage hose on the picnic table while they were packing up. Knowing this, I want to be sure that all the dirt and germs on the picnic table came from us and not the people before us.

Table cloth. (see above) A table cloth after you use the Lysol wipes gives great peace of mind and helps make the table surface a bit more even (think of the spaces between the picnic table boards). Again, we find them at the Dollar Store.

Can opener, vegetable peeler, aluminum foil, cheese grater, tongs, a large sharp knife with a protective sleeve, a strainer/colander, spatula, and plastic containers for leftovers. These essentials are easy to overlook when packing until you get to the site to open the can of beans, and call to your partner, "Where is the can opener?" To avoid this issue, I have duplicates of all the items listed here that we use just for camping. They stay in the large kitchen items container in my trailer year-round. That way there is no way to forget them.

Broom and mop. For the first-timers, this item is often overlooked and underappreciated – until you forget it at home. We use the broom several times a day and use the flat mop with the disposable wipes at least every other day if not more frequently. We have a set that we leave in the trailer.

Laundry clothesline. We have a separate rope line specifically for drying clothes. Because we are often doing large loads of laundry while camping, we have several long ropes. These are wrapped around empty water bottles for storage.

To make the best use of real estate (tree supports), we will wrap the line to go out on one side of the tree and come back on the other side of the tree (2 lines in parallel). If needed, we will also do a second line lower down, to give us two tiers. But that is only needed when we are drying 5 loads of shorts and shirts.

Even if you do not plan to do any laundry on the trip, you will need a laundry line to dry towels and swimsuits between uses. If you are going to a campground with limited or no trees, remember to bring a collapsible laundry drying rack.

Pain relief pills and first aid kit. I put a dozen or so pain pills (Aspirin, Tylenol, Advil) in zip lock bags or empty pill bottles to have on hand. Label all containers and bags clearly. I also pack ointment, band-aids, rubbing alcohol, hydrogen peroxide, bug bite kit, and other things like tweezers. Things can happen out there.

Camping chairs. Unless it is raining, you will probably be spending the majority of your time outdoors.

Let's get real. The picnic table is made of wood slabs, which have never been defined as comfortable.

The only chairs you will be sitting on for almost your entire stay are the camping chairs you brought. Consider your camping chairs an investment.

I recommend ones with a side table attached, which makes it super convenient for drinks, your phone, etc., and it won't shift or topple over like a separate side table could.

Invest in the best and most durable chairs you can. You will be sitting in them more than you care to admit.

Duct Tape. I do not travel ANYWHERE without duct tape, regardless if I am camping, or traveling by plane to a house or resort. Red Green has called it "the handyman's secret weapon", and he is correct. We have used it for emergency awning repair and emergency roof leak repair, emergency suitcase repair, in addition to a million other possibilities. If there is an emergency, more often than not, duct tape will be involved in the solution.

PVC Pipe. For frequent marshmallow roasters, it works great to keep the marshmallow sticks together and off the dirt. Cap each end with piping on one end and use some tough and durable cloth to wrap around the other end. Use a thick elastic to keep it sealed tight.

Dry Lubricant. We have several windows that slide open (not crank out), and they have a reputation for getting stuck part way up or down which is super frustrating. We use a dry lubricant, available from most hardware stores in the automotive section. It makes getting them opened and closed much easier.

GATHERING AROUND THE FIRE
IN A FIRE BAN

Propane firepits. This is completely optional, but it is nice to have.

For the die-hard fire pit people, I get it. You need to have a roaring fire every night or it's not camping. But when there is a fire ban (and in many places, there often is a fire ban for at least half of each summer), if you do not have a propane firepit you have no fire at all.

We have also found it useful when you just want to hang out around the fire for a little bit. It's late and the kids want smores but you don't want to have to commit to having a fire for the next 4 hours. Turn on the firepit and when you have had enough, presto, it's off. As a guideline, we can have it on for about an hour a night for 2 weeks before the 20-pound propane tank runs out, which is cheaper than buying 8 dollars' worth of firewood each night.

OVERNIGHTING TIPS WHEN MULTI-DAY TRAVELLING

Since we travel for a month or more at a time, our destination campsite is often 2 or more days from our home. This means we have to figure out how to handle the overnight stop(s) on the road.

The first thing we do is figure out where the destination for each day will be and how many miles we plan to cover.

Then the figure out our camping options.

A free App that was recommended to use by many people who travel in their vans full-time is called Overlander. To use, you look on the map where you want to go and it pulls up all the locations in its database with campgrounds, rest areas, dump stations, and gas stations in the area. All the information and reviews are provided by other app users. Feel free to add your location feedback as well.

Frequently when we stay overnight in a store parking lot that allows overnight camping, they leave on their very bright parking lot lights ALL night.

If you plan to camp there, you need blackout curtains. Otherwise, you might think you are sleeping directly next to the sun.

I made blackout curtains by cutting to size and hemming larger blackout curtains (straight stitch doubled or tripled over on top and bottom) that were made for longer windows. I used clip-on ring hooks on the segments that did not have rings already done. It took about a weekend to finish this at a cost of about $80.

WINTERIZING YOUR TRAILER
& AVOIDING UNWANTED SQUATTERS

If you live in a climate where it gets below freezing over the winter, you need to winterize your trailer before storing it for the season.

Empty all the water out and replace it with RV antifreeze. This is NOT the same as regular antifreeze, and they CANNOT be interchanged. It MUST be RV plumbing antifreeze. It is pink and smells like bourbon.

For reasons that cannot be explained, you can only get the RV antifreeze in 1 or 2.5-gallon containers. That means you will need more than 1 container of the stuff (we need 5 gallons for our trailer or 2 of the 2.5-gallon size) to winterize the RV. Both the inbound water lines and the outgoing lines need to be filled with the RV antifreeze to prevent the lines from cracking in the cold.

The fridge and freezer should be left open over the winter storage to allow airflow and reduce the chances of getting mold in the fridge from condensation. Unfortunately, this one we know from experience.

To discourage critters from setting up shop for the winter in your RV, we have several precautionary steps while in storage.

1 – Dryer sheets – the strongest odor ones you can find. We use a full box throughout the trailer. Mice don't like the chemicals in them.

2 – Peppermint Cotton Balls. Mice (and spiders) don't like the smell of peppermint essential oil. Soak cotton balls with several drops of peppermint essential oil and place around the trailer.

Both of these should be placed in both open and closed spaces, including drawers.

3- Take out all blankets and sleeping bags, and anything warm from the trailer. It is a draw for the mice to take up shop there if they do get in.

BEFORE DRIVING AWAY –
AVOID REPEATING OUR MISTAKES

We have forgotten or had issues with every one of the following items. To prevent you from the same experiences, I am providing a quick reminder.

Make sure the step to get into the trailer is up. Check the passenger mirror before you hit the gas. Someone could have gone in at the last minute and forgot to put up the step. If you destroy the step you are not going anywhere. It happened to us. A 6-day trip came to an abrupt halt before it started and it cost us $300 to get a new step.

Double-check that the awning is locked in place. It can look close to locked and not be locked, especially in older models. If it comes open on the highway, the wind will destroy it.

Make sure all the doors are locked. You do not need to have a door to swing open on a bump at 60 miles per hour.

Make sure all the windows are closed. Not only will having the windows open increase drag, it will also coat the interior with dust.

In the same vein, look up and make sure the roof vents are closed.

Make sure the water heater and water pump are turned off. It is not recommended to have either in use when traveling on the road.

Check that you took down the clothesline. Once the clothes are taken off the line that thing goes into camouflage mode. We have left it behind more than once.

Ensure everything that has any chance of falling is either secured in place or on the floor. If you entered our trailer on a travel day, there is maybe 2 square feet of unused floor space. Everything, from toiletries to water filters is secured in place with larger and heavier things on the floor.

Each and every time I go in the trailer, the last thing I do is ensure the fridge and freezer and closed and fully latched, and then double-check (by hitting the doors), that all cabinets and drawers are latched and closed.

Consider the trailer to be going through the equivalent of a substantial earthquake for the entire travel time, so secure everything accordingly.

RESERVING YOUR CAMPSITE – AN ART, A SCIENCE, & TIMING

You may think that you are the only people who have considered camping this year. I have some bad news for you. Camping is extremely popular, and that little patch of dirt/pavement/grass with a picnic table and firepit can be considered a premium.

The days of assuming that you can just drive down the road and find a campground with lots of available sites are long over. The number of new campgrounds has not matched the increased number of people camping. The best campgrounds and the best sites will fill up fast.

This means that if you want to be assured a campsite, you should reserve it. Every campground has a different date that they accept reservations. Some are 90 days, 120 days, 6 months, 9 months and some are a year or even up to 2 years in advance. If the reservation window opens 9 months in advance, it means that you are booking for your July trip in October of the previous year.

If there is a campground that you want, booking it sooner than later is ideal. Whenever possible, we will book the site as soon as the reservation window opens for the dates we are looking for. Literally. If the window opens at 8 am on March 1, for example, we are hitting the reserve button for the site at 8 am on March 1. Not 8:01, but 8:00.

That means you need to figure out which site you want before the reservation window opens. The better you prepare for this, like everything else in camping, the happier you will be when you arrive.

You also need to know the cancellation and change policies before you book. Some have no charge with enough notice, some won't refund anything after you book, and there is everything in-between. Make sure you know your cancellation options before you hand over your hard-earned money, especially when you are booking many months in advance.

I know many people want to wait until they have their vacation dates approved. But often by then most if not all of the reservable sites are taken. If the cancellation polies are fairly flexible and affordable, we risk the $20 cancellation fee to get a reservation secured when there are good sites still available.

Also, the weekends fill up faster than butter melts on a hot grill, so if your trip is over a weekend, keep that in mind.

When selecting a site, if the campground has pictures, and provides a campground map, check them out. Also, look for campsite reviews from independent sites. That will give you another perspective. All campgrounds are not equal and all sites in the campground are not equal. We will even check out the campsites and campgrounds on Google earth to get a better idea of layouts.

Items we consider when choosing a campground and the campsite:

Does it have power, water/sewer and does that matter? Can you drink the water in the campground (not all are potable)?

How far to a town with grocery stores and gas (especially if it is for longer stays)? Your wilderness site might be great, but if it takes 40 minutes one-way to buy food and you forgot to pack bread, the shine of the location might wear off in a hurry.

How far is it from a water source for refilling the tank? (if we don't have water hook ups)

How far from the washrooms? Ideally you are a couple sites away, but not right next the washroom. Washrooms can be double edged sword. They are often lit up at night, which is not great for sleeping and there can sometimes be smell issues, depending on the campground. And there is the increased foot traffic from everyone else going to the washrooms. You also do not want the washrooms so far away that you need to plan 30 minutes in advance for the grand trip. (We have been known to ride our bikes there if we are further away.) You are looking for goldilocks distances.

The same goes for garbage bins. Not so far that taking out the garbage (which you will do daily) becomes the trek of the century, and not so close that you enjoy the smells from the bins from your site. You also have increased foot traffic from everyone else going to the garbage if you are nearby.

Does the site have trees and do they look like they will give shade? If you want to do solar, you are looking for full sun- a little shade or cloud really drops off the effectiveness of the solar panels. If you do not want to roast outside, you are looking for some shade for relief.

How much privacy do the trees and/or bushes provide? A thousand thin tree sticks with high branches may give shade but not a lick of privacy. Does the site have anything between you and the next site? We have seen campgrounds with the next site right beside you, but have a 12-foot wall of cedars that give much more privacy, even though you don't have the physical distance between the sites.

How large is the campsite? We have a trailer over 30 feet long, plus the tow vehicle. Will it fit both? How wide is the site? It is long and narrow, or will it fit our kitchen tables, and all the chairs?

How much space between our site and the guys next to us? Some sites have 20 feet between them. Others have 1 foot between them, when you are staring at the wall of the trailer beside you and they could see you changing at night and can give you tips on your décor from their window, especially in some RV parks.

Group camping sites and double sites tend to be noisier with multiple families having a great party/reunion and we try to avoid the sites immediately next to those.

Does it have any other amenities that you really want, such as wi-fi (extremely important for us if we can get it), cell coverage, pools, bike parks, hiking trails from the campground, mini-golf, games room, laundry room, general store, restaurant, paved sites, playgrounds, lake access or beach?

You may not get your full wish list every time, but the more information you use before you commit, the closer the site will meet your expectations.

EASY CAMPING RECIPES

As a bonus, here are some of our well-used camping recipes. Yes, I know that these are super simple, but really camping is enough work without having to mimic Julia Child in the forest.

These recipes are relatively fast, decently nutritious (with obvious exceptions), and simple enough that even if you can't cook, you can still master these.

I have also listed obvious and simple meals, just to spur on your ideas. This also is to remind you that even simple stuff can be great outdoors. Anytime you can eat outside without a bug landing in your food is a good meal.

Tasty Oatmeal

Here's a secret: You do not need to waste your money on instant oatmeal. If you use quick oats, it is instant oatmeal. Add hot water, stir and within 5 seconds you have oatmeal. Seriously.

Add you a few tasty and nutritious items and BAM! Tasty oatmeal. The biggest weakness of oatmeal is that it is mushy. I add a crunchy granola topping to give it balance.

- oatmeal (quick oats, not rolled oats)
- very hot water
- flavorings and sweeteners: cinnamon, brown sugar, or maple syrup.
- healthy add-ins: chia seeds, ground flaxseed, collagen powder.
- fruit of your choice, berries work really well. Favorites are strawberry, blueberry and banana mix. Also, strawberry and peaches are lovely.
- crunchy topper, such as granola or bran buds. I prefer granola. (about 1 tbsp)
- milk or alternative milk (we like almond coconut milk blend)

Mix in the flavorings of your choice. We add about ½ tsp of cinnamon but add it to your taste. If you can smell it when you mix it in, you will be able to taste it. Other flavors that work well vanilla or pumpkin pie spice. (yes, I know you didn't think to bring it otherwise, but because you read this before you left, so you can decide before you leave if you want to bring it along).

Add the healthy stuff if you have it. Add hot water until it gets to the thickness you like. Top with the fruit and then the granola. Add milk to surround it all. That's it!

BBQ Corn

This method lets you make corn without the hassle of trying to husk it in advance and without having to boil a huge pot of water. After we tried this the first time, there was no going back to the medieval ways of water boil method for us.

- corn
- butter and salt

Here's the trick. Do NOT peel the corn. Leave it in the husk. Cut off the extra hairs on top and the extra bottom husk if either is too long, but do not peel. Ideally, you have not even opened it a bit to see the inside at all.

Put on the bottom rack of BBQ on medium heat. Turn over every few minutes until it is charred on all sides. Normally it takes about 10 minutes. When they are a little soft when you squeeze them, and all sides have had the direct heat they are ready. Remove from grill.

The corn has basically been steaming in the husks and they will be very hot. It is easy to burn your hand from the heat, so be careful. It should peel much easier than when the husks were raw and all those little corn hairs refused to come off.

Serve with butter and salt. That's it!

Quick note: Do not make these inside or near your trailer or your house. Sometimes the exterior husk often catches fire for a bit if there are a lot of husk layers.

Personalized Pizzas

Most portable BBQs are too small to support a full-sized pizza, and I don't like to use to oven in the trailer because it is too small, too close to the gas source and heats up the trailer, which is something I do not need on a hot summer evening.

- naan bread or pita bread or individual pizza crusts
- spaghetti sauce
- mozzarella cheese
- cheddar cheese
- toppings of your choice

Spread spaghetti sauce on your individual pizza crusts of your choice. Grate the cheese and top each pizza with the cheese and toppings of your choice. Place on the top rack of your BBQ if you have one.

If you don't have a top rack, put a layer of aluminum foil on the lower rack, spray it with PAM to prevent sticking before putting the pizzas on to cook. You need to reduce the amount of direct heat to prevent the crusts from burning on the bottom.

We serve with baked beans, veggies, and dip.

That's it!

Burrito Wraps

Ok, so this makes a larger mess than most of my camping recipes, but it is well received by the entire family. Serves 5.

- tortillas, 1 per person
- 1 can of baked beans in tomato sauce
- 1.25 cups of rice
- ½ pound of meat – any of your choice and/or mushrooms
- garlic
- 1 onion, chopped

Other optional add-ins:

- avocado
- shredded cheddar cheese
- onions
- coleslaw
- sour cream
- salsa
- peppers (any color – green, red, orange or yellow)
- red onions

Cook the rice like you normally would. If you want extra flavor, add ½ tsp chili powder and/or ½ tsp cumin and/or ½ tsp chicken bouillon or ½ a package of onion soup mix.

Cook the meat and/or mushrooms. Add the chopped onion and 1-2 cloves of chopped garlic. If you want more flavor, you can add, chili paste and/or cumin and/or Clubhouse TexMex Seasoning.

Heat the beans.

Warm up the tortilla shells.

Now assemble. On the tortilla shell, along the centre put cheese on the bottom, avocado next if you have it. Next is rice, then meat, then beans. Top with the veggies if you want them, then top with salsa and sour cream. Fold over the ends and roll it over to form a burrito.

The order of ingredients is the difference between good and great. You preferably want the top and bottom to be cream-based (cheese, or sour cream, avocado). If you put on salsa, make sure it is next to the sour cream to offset it and add a zing to the cream.

That's it!

Ultimate Homemade Fries

- potatoes (1-2.5 per person)
- olive oil (about 2 tbsp)
- McCormick's Vegetable seasoning
- McCormick's TexMex seasoning
- garlic powder or crushed garlic (about 1 tbsp if using crushed garlic)
- rosemary (about 1 tbsp)
- salt & pepper

Cut the potatoes into bite-size cubes (just under an inch by an inch). Put in a large bowl, add the olive oil, toss to coat all sides. Add the seasonings until it looks like all sides are lightly spiced. If you don't have the seasoning mix, the garlic and rosemary work really well on their own as well. Or use chili powder by itself if you want a change.

The aluminum foil sections should be about 12 inches long. Roll up all four edges of the rectangle twice to make a mini pan. Put the potatoes in the foil and keep it at one layer. Repeat with multiple foil sections until all potatoes are accounted for. I put the foil pans on a solid cutting board and use the board to support everything in transport. Then slide the foil packets onto the BBQ.

Cook in BBQ at med-high until soft when you pierce the potatoes with a fork. It usually takes us about 30 minutes. That's it!

Peanut Butter Smore-Like Snacks

Using peanut butter gives a bit of protein to help reduce the blood sugar spike and give an interesting twist. The Nutella and chocolate chip blend allow you to get the chocolatey element without a huge chocolate commitment or having to sit there forever waiting for the chocolate to melt.

- crackers – can use graham (traditional), ritz, or just soda crackers in a pinch
- peanut butter
- nutella
- chocolate chips (milk chocolate is preferable) (traditional method is to use a whole chocolate bar, but I'm not buying 450 full-sized chocolate bars for a month-long trip)
- marshmallows

Spread peanut butter on one cracker, Nutella on the other and sprinkle with chocolate chips.

Heat marshmallows over the fire. When done, place between the 2 crackers.

That's it!

Dessert Cones

This is simple, and a super yummy.

- marshmallows – cut up the big ones or use the mini ones
- peanuts or peanut butter
- bananas, sliced
- chocolate chips
- raspberries or blueberries if you have them
- any other fun ingredients, such as peanut butter chips or M&Ms
- waffle cones

Put all ingredients into the waffle cone. Wrap in tin foil and heat on a grate over the fire. When gooey, it's done.

That's it!

Ultimate Egg Sandwich

Per serving:

- 1 egg
- 1 sausage patty or bacon
- ¼ of an onion slice
- maple syrup
- 2 slices of toast or english muffins

On a griddle or frying pan, cook up the bacon or sausage and the onion in the bacon fat.

Cook the egg to your liking, whichever you prefer. Put the toast on the BBQ if you don't have a functioning toaster.

Assembly: On your toast put the meat and onion. Top with the egg. Add a splash of maple syrup if you have it. Finish with salt and pepper to taste and the other piece of bread.

That's it!

Roast Beef Pinwheels

- 8 roast beef (or ham or chicken) slices
- 2 tbsp mustard or honey mustard or Dijon mustard
- 8 provolone cheese slices (or cheddar/mozzarella)
- 1 pkg of refrigerated crescent rolls
- 1/2 cup diced red pepper and/or red onions

Unroll crescent rolls and cut along perforations (after sufficient struggling to get the package to pop)

Spread each roll with mustard.

Sprinkle with red pepper/onions.

Top with meat and cheese slices

Roll it from longest pointy end, so that on the end it looks like a cinnamon roll with meat and cheese in it.

Put on greased aluminum foil on BBQ on medium heat.

Cook until the rolls are completely cooked through and brown, about 15 minutes. Can serve with extra mustard if you love mustard.

Addictive Granola Bars

These are seriously addictive. I make them before we leave for a snack on the road, but they could easily be made at the campsite as well. I make an extra batch so that there is enough left for the trip. Otherwise the family will secretly polish them off before we leave the driveway.

- 1 egg
- 1/2 cup butter or a combination of ¼ cup butter and 1/4 cup coconut oil, melted
- 1/2 cup sugar
- 1/3 cup cocoa
- 1 tbsp instant coffee
- 1 tsp vanilla
- 1/2 cup shredded coconut
- 1 cup graham wafer crumbs
- 1/4 cup peanut butter
- 1 1/3 cup oats
- 1/4 cup walnuts or other nut of choice, chopped
- 1/2 cup chocolate chips in mix, plus about 1.5 cups for on top

Mix all wet ingredients together, then add dry ingredients until all is moist. If it looks dry, add more butter.

Spread evenly on a cookie sheet that is lined with foil (spray with non-stick spray or with butter) or use parchment paper. I use a rolling pin to make it all even, but you can use your hands or anything else you want to make it flat and about 1/4 inch thick.

Cook at 350 F for 10 minutes.

Granola Bars ...continued.

Pull from the oven and top with remaining chocolate chips. Put back in oven for 5 minutes to let them melt – they will still hold their shape, so don't expect them to spread out on their own.

Remove from oven and use a knife to spread the chocolate chips over the top.

Let cool and cut into bars. Hide from everyone until you are ready to have them devoured.

Easy Peaches and Berries Cobbler (or Apples)

- 6 cups of peaches or apples, peeled and sliced about ¼ inch thick
- 2 cups berries of your choice – blackberries, strawberries, raspberries and/or blueberries
- 1 tbsp lemon juice
- ½ cup sugar
- 1 tsp cinnamon
- ¼ tsp cardamom (if you have it – really adds to the flavor)
- 3 tbsp cornstarch (you will need to plan for this from home to remember to bring a bit)
- 1 pkg of refrigerated biscuits or crescent rolls

Mix together everything except the crescent rolls and cook over low-medium heat on stove until the fruit softens, about 10 minutes.

Put mixture into a baking dish or skillet proof pan, or anything with high enough sides that it won't spill over in cooking but can handle high heat.

Open the refrigerated rolls (after sufficient struggling and grunting to get it open). Top the mixture with the rolls. Sprinkle on top of the rolls with melted butter and sugar if you want to get fancy.

Cook at 350 F or medium heat on BBQ until the rolls are cooked and brown, about 15 minutes. If you have ice cream somewhere in the freezer, add a scoop on top.

Other Meal Ideas to Eat in the Middle of Nowhere

Spaghetti (although it is messier for clean-up)

Hot Dogs

Sandwiches or Wraps – Tuna, Ham, Chicken, Cheese, Egg, Peanut Butter

Sausages or smokies

Beans and Cheese Toast

Eggs and Bacon or Sausage

Pancakes

Salads:

- Basic Garden
- Pasta
- Potato
- Coleslaw

Toast (you can toast a half dozen slices at once on the BBQ)

Chili

If you enjoyed these recipes, you can find all my best recipes that you can master in a campsite (76 recipes to be exact) in my book also available on Amazon,
RV Camping Cookbook: Family Favorites Easy and Tasty Recipes to Enjoy by the Campfire With the Kids

ABOUT THE AUTHOR

Sara Bowton has been camping since her teens. She started her camping experiences in tents, then moved up to tent-trailers and has been camping in full-sized trailers for over 10 years. Sara with her husband, three children and 3 dogs in tow have camped around North America each year for over 2 decades.

They have camped in all conditions, often for over a month at a time, using fully and partially serviced campsites, unserviced campsites and rest stops. They have camped several years for 5 weeks straight using only unserviced campsites. This was with the full family and pets for the entire time. They managed to finish the trip without a divorce or the near-death of anyone.

She also loves baking and makes a mean set of triple chocolate cookies.

ONE LAST THING...

THANK YOU for taking the time to read this book.

I hope that the tips make your future camping trips much easier and enjoyable.

If you think of additional camping questions, please feel free to email me. I will do my best to answer and may include the response in future updates to help others. My goal is to help you enjoy camping to the best of my ability.

If you enjoyed this book or found it useful, I'd be very grateful if you'd post a short review on Amazon. Your support really does make a difference and I read all the reviews personally so I can get your feedback and make this book even better.

If you'd like to leave a review then all you need to do is click the review link on this book's page on Amazon.

Thank you again for your support and Happy Travels!

Sara Bowton

Made in the USA
Middletown, DE
27 September 2021